Home on Purpose

SHARON HINES

Free Printable Resources

This book comes with **FREE Printable Resources** designed to kickstart creating your home on purpose. The resources include:
- Daily Routine Chart
- Cleaning Schedule
- DIY cleaner recipe cards. Print these as labels to put on your cleaning bottles, or use them as recipe cards in your home management binder.
- Step-by-step decluttering guide with sorting labels.

Get your guide at sharonehines.com/ResourceGuide so you can implement them as you read the book.

Copyright © 2015 Sharon Hines

All rights reserved. This book or any portion thereof may not be reproduced or used in any manner whatsoever without express written permission except for the use of brief quotations in a book review. To obtain permission, email sharon@sharonehines.com with the subject line "Permission Request."

The information in this book is heavily based on personal experience and anecdotal evidence. Although the author has made every effort to ensure that the information in this book was correct at press time, the author does not assume any liability to any party for any loss, damage, or disruption caused by errors or omissions. This information in this book is to be used at your own risk.

Cover design by Rebecacovers on Fiverr.com
Editing by Penoaks Publishing
Formatting by Suzy Taylor Oakley at suzyoakley.com
Photography by Sharon Hines

Disclosure: This book contains affiliate links. This means that if you click on an affiliate link and make a purchase, I will make a small commission (at no additional cost to you). It is important to me that you know I only recommend products or brands that I use and/or trust. I'm disclosing this information in accordance with the Federal Trade Commission's 16 CFR, Part 255 – "Guides Concerning the Use of Endorsements and Testimonials in Advertising."

For my husband Matt
and our daughter Hannah

Table of Contents

INTRODUCTION | 9

PART 1: ELEVATING YOUR MINDSET
    Chapter 1: *Defining Home* | 13
    Chapter 2: *Make Yourself at Home* | 17
    Chapter 3: *The Dish Towel* | 19
    Chapter 4: *More Than a Sitting Room* | 22
    Chapter 5: *The Comforts of Home* | 25
    Chapter 6: *It's Family Tradition* | 28
    Chapter 7: *What's The Occasion?* | 34
    Chapter 8: *Conclusion – The Wanting* | 36

PART 2: CLEARING THE CLUTTER
    Chapter 9: *The Importance of Organizing* | 39
    Chapter 10: *The 4-Part Decluttering Method* | 44
    Chapter 11: *5 Simple Storage Tips* | 52
    Chapter 12: *A Place for Everything* | 54
    Chapter 13: *Staying Organized* | 60

PART 3: KEEPING IT CLEAN
    Chapter 14: *Greasy Stove Tops* | 65
    Chapter 15: *The Goldilocks Approach to Cleaning* | 68
    Chapter 16: *Creating a Cleaning Routine* | 71
    Chapter 17: *Cleaning Tips and Tricks* | 75

PART 4: TIME AND ENERGY
- Chapter 18: *Beating Procrastination* | 81
- Chapter 19: *Establishing Priorities* | 87
- Chapter 20: *Taking Back Time* | 89
- Chapter 21: *Energy Crisis* | 98
- Chapter 22: *Tips for Taking Care of Yourself* | 102

PART 5: OVERCOMING DECORATING DILEMMAS
- Chapter 23: *Facing Your Fears* | 111
- Chapter 24: *Smart Decorating Advice* | 113
- Chapter 25: *9 Practical Tips for Defining Your Style* | 116
- Chapter 26: *5 Budget Decorating Ideas* | 121
- Chapter 27: *Overcoming Indecision* | 124
- Chapter 28: 8 Kid-Friendly Design Ideas / 128
- Chapter 29: *Space Planning* | 131
- Chapter 30: *Decorating Tips and Tricks* | 136
- Chapter 31: *Personalizing Your Home Decor* | 142
- Chapter 32: *Finding Home* | 149

Acknowledgements

It was only recently that I realized my passion and know-how for creating a home with purpose stemmed from my upbringing. Little did I know that as a young girl who was made to sit at the table with her brother and sisters for dinner instead of watch TV, or as a teenager who thought her bedtime and curfew were both too early, or as a young adult who decided to strike out on her own too soon, that I would one day look back with such appreciation for my childhood home.

Mom and Dad, this book would not be possible without all your provision, love, and support over the years. Thank you.

I also want to thank my brother and sisters. I've lived a richer life and am a better person for having done life with you. Everyone should be so lucky as to grow up and consider your siblings your favorite people. Words cannot express how much I love you and appreciate your support through the years.

And I have to thank the women in my life who have modeled strength, independence, perseverance, and faith. I'm not sure I would have had the determination to pursue my dreams of being an author without their influence. To name a few – my grandmother Nonna, Aunt Barbara, Aunt Marilyn, Aunt Becky, my cousin Kristen, my mom and sisters, and my daughter, Hannah.

Last, but certainly not least, I want to say thank you to my husband, Matt. Thank you for loving me just as I am, for your support on all of my endeavors, and for your encouragement to pursue my dreams.

Introduction

Your world is hectic. You're sleep deprived, forgetful, and always in a hurry. The good news is it's still possible to be present and enjoy this stage of life. In other words, you can live in your home on purpose.

But what I've found in my experience as a professional organizer and lifestyle blogger is that many of us just aren't quite sure how or where to start, typically because of overwhelm from one of these common obstacles:

Mindset – Our understanding of what a home truly is and how our home lives affect every other area of our lives.

Clutter – The mental and emotional clutter that occurs from stress and physical clutter.

Time – Feeling like you're just too busy with momming to maintain your household. Procrastination has become your new best frenemy.

Energy – A lack of the energy and motivation needed to find what works and put it into practice, because see above.

Decorating Dilemmas – Feeling like having nice things or a pretty home has to wait.

Before I go any further, I want you to look back at the last sentence before the list you just finished reading starts. See the word common? You are not alone.

If I've seen it once, I've seen it a million times. When even one of these areas are out of order, so is your home, and when your home is out of order, you drown in overwhelm. I wish I could wave a magic wand or wiggle my nose and make all of your stress disappear. Since I can't do that, I'm going to do the only thing I know to do – teach.

This book will draw from my experiences and share what I've learned about creating space for a mindful lifestyle, both in my own life and in the lives of many clients. Each part of the book will address one of the five obstacles and provide practical help and resources for overcoming them. I've also included a **free Printable Resource Guide** that consists of – a daily routine chart, a cleaning schedule, DIY cleaner recipe cards, a step-by-step decluttering guide and sorting labels. *(Get your tool* *kit at sharonehines.com/ResourceGuide, or by clicking on the links provided in the resource pages of each section in the book.)*

I recommend reading this book from beginning to end, because you just may discover a tip or nugget of wisdom that you hadn't heard before. However, if you've got a handle on a topic, pick up with the first area of concern, then work your way through the rest of the book. However you choose to approach the book, I am confident that, if you do the work, you'll be well on your way to creating a home on purpose.

PART 1
Elevating Your Mindset

"A home is a whole world, made up of not only memories and real life, but of plans for the future, of enthusiasms and passions."

Christiane de Nicolay-Mazery

CHAPTER 1

Defining Home

"Home is the nicest word there is."

Laura Ingalls Wilder

I MOVED A LOT as a young adult, staying no more than a year in any one place. The only constant in my ever-changing world was the address on my driver's license, Mom and Dad's address, until one day when I got pulled over.

While being issued a ticket for "failure to change address," I tried to tell the officer that my parents' house was my permanent address...It's where I received my mail.

But, as the officer explained, the law defines your permanent address as the place where you lay your head at night. And that's pretty much how I lived – working, volunteering, and hanging out with friends until it was time for bed.

Home was just where I slept at night.

Over the years, my definition of home has changed a lot. It's not simply my mailing address or the place where I lay down at night. What I've come to realize over the years is this:

> *"Home is a sacred place, not to be taken lightly. Whether you are clearing the clutter, re-decorating, or renovating — let the intention behind the design be from the heart. Create spaces for your family that will help them thrive. Home is comfortable, inspiring, and it's where life happens."*
>
> Joanna Gaines

Let's think about that for a moment. At first, I thought the word "sacred" was a little strong, maybe even misused, but after reading the definition, I agree.

> **sacred** – *Connected to God or dedicated to a religious purpose.*

Our homes are a place set apart from the outside world for rest and renewal, in turn allowing us to share our gifts and talents with others. That is indeed a religious work.

That means that you have a great responsibility, a high calling. You are creating a space that nurtures your household, builds them up, and causes them to thrive.

> **thrive** – *synonyms – flourish, prosper, bloom, blossom, advance, succeed*

So if I were to dig a little deeper, I think I kept my parents' address not just because I moved a lot, but because it was my sacred place.

It was the place where I was surrounded by the people and things I loved the most. It held meaning and memories. It was where my parents prepared me for the future. It was my foundation, giving me the strength and courage to pursue dreams and live the life I imagined.

Mom and Dad's house, my childhood home, determined what I wanted in a home. Once I realized that, my mindset shifted, and I set out to recreate that for my household. That is what I want for you – to grab hold of all that home is and create yours with purpose.

Chapter 2

Make Yourself at Home

I NEVER UNPACKED. Any time I traveled, I never unpacked. Whether I was staying in a hotel or with someone, I kept everything contained within my luggage, taking out only what I needed and putting it right back again. I literally lived out of my suitcase.

Nor did I take advantage of the amenities. I viewed everything around me as "theirs." But not unpacking and settling in made me feel anxious, like I didn't have roots or a place to call my own.

So the last time I traveled, I set out my toiletries and put my clothes in drawers, which made me feel much more at home.

What I've learned is this – Treating your space as temporary keeps you from fully living and from fully resting. Home isn't limited to a house you own. Home can be a bedroom, a rental, a hotel, or guest quarters.

So wherever you may live, unpack, so to speak, and make yourself at home. Set out photos, hang pictures, buy accessories. You're not wasting your time or money; you're investing it in your home, in your sense of well-being.

CHAPTER 3

The Dish Towel That Changed Everything

We tend to treat the ordinary days of our lives like they're something to be dreaded or escaped. I felt that way too, until I encountered the dish towel that changed everything…

Every time I passed by the kitchen, the dish towel hanging over the cabinet door caught my eye. There was something about it — the easy way it hung, its folds and wrinkles — that I found comforting. I knew

there was a life lesson waiting in that dish towel, but I couldn't quite put my finger on it.

Then one day I read an analogy that compared life to being at Disney. You wait in a long line, *for a long time*, as it slowly moves along. Finally, your turn comes and you step out of the line and onto a ride that lasts all of a few exhilarating minutes. Then you do it all over again. After reading that, the lesson in the dish towel began to unfold...

I used to despise the long lines of life, the seasons of waiting. I wished away the days of waiting because I thought life was all about the ride. Now I realize life is about both, *but mostly the waiting*. That's where faith, trust, dependence, and preparation for the ride happens.

Waiting is a place of rest, a place to enjoy the ordinary, and it's a place where I can find comfort in a simple dish towel.

That is the mindset we need to adopt concerning our homes. The chores, the routine, the messes, and even dish towels are symbols of an ordinary, everyday life.

If we learn to find beauty in the ordinary, then we will find comfort in it. *That* is extraordinary. In the next few chapters, I'll share some ideas that will help you add a little something extra to the ordinary.

CHAPTER 4

More Than a Sitting Room

Your home will be more nurturing if you use it to suit your lifestyle.

Let's take my breakfast room as an example. Not only does my family not eat breakfast at the same time, but everyone just grabs something to go on their way out the door.

However, the breakfast room gets a lot of morning sunlight and opens to the back patio. So, when I started thinking about what I wanted my morning routine to look like, I decided the breakfast room would be better suited as a sitting room where I could enjoy the natural light and ease into the day. Once that decision was made, a design plan fell into place.

As I work on turning my breakfast room into a sitting room, I dream of more than just a sitting room. **I dream of a way of life –** a life in which I walk through a set of French doors onto my back porch and stretch under the sun. Then I walk back through those French doors, *leaving them wide open*, and I linger… just long enough to prepare for the day ahead.

By the way, I don't have a set of French doors …*yet*, and there aren't very many flowers in the backyard either, but that isn't stopping me from using the space in a way that suits my lifestyle.

I'm reminded of my teaching days when students would come to me because so-and-so wouldn't play with them. My advice was either to jump in and start playing or to find a different group of friends to play with.

The moral of the story is this – Don't wait to be invited to live the life you want. If you like to read, set up a cozy reading nook. If you're a crafter, set aside a craft area. Whether you repurpose a room or convert a closet, create spaces that foster the lifestyle you want.

Chapter 5

The Comforts of Home

When I think of spreading my wings and flying, I picture being satisfied, fulfilled, and at complete peace. Being at home should bring us that kind of comfort. So, let's talk about how we can achieve that in our homes. I'll let you in on a little secret – <u>It's not about the stuff so much as it is about the setting.</u> With that in mind, here are 8 ways to make your house feel like home.

Scent – Whether that's the smell of dinner cooking, a freshly cleaned home, or your favorite candle, scents evoke comfort.

Smile – at each other. Laugh together. There's nothing as satisfying and healing as laughter.

Structure – We all thrive on some semblance of structure. A routine makes us feel safe.

Reduce stress – by having a system in place. Menu planning, calendars, daily planners, and home management binders all help reduce stress.

Organization – Having a place for everything and everything in its place brings a sense of order. When things are in order, we feel calm.

Space – Everyone needs a space to call their own, to retreat to. Mr. Hines likes to retreat to the chaise lounge and read in the quiet of our bedroom. We use a bedroom as a teen lounge so that our daughter and her friends have a place to giggle and talk about boys. And I love cuddling up under a blanket in the living room.

Personalize – with photos, mementos, scrapbooks, monograms, and personal items like children's artwork and childhood belongings…. Anything that has meaning to your family.

Traditions – Establishing traditions is a great way to bond and form lasting memories.

We're going to go into more detail on many of these comforts of home later in the book, but for now, let's talk about traditions.

CHAPTER 6

It's Family Tradition

TRADITIONS ARE A GREAT WAY to bond as a family and build lasting memories, and over the years my family has established quite a few. Some of them stem from my childhood, some were started in more recent years, and others I look forward to starting. Hopefully these traditions will spark some ideas for you and your family.

Fall Family Potluck – If it's not the year for Thanksgiving with my side of the family, we have a family dinner *(man, do we eat good that day!)*, draw names for Christmas, play games, and enjoy each other's company.

Oscar Party – A few years ago we started getting together with friends to watch the Academy Awards. It's a fun excuse to eat, drink, and be merry.

Back to School Dinner – I recently started this tradition with friends. It's so nice to look forward to a home-cooked meal at the end of a long first day of school.

Mother's Day Beach Trip – All I ask for Mother's Day is a good book and a chair on the beach. We've been doing this for at least ten years now.

Annual Photo – My mom and I share a birthday. So every year we take a picture of us smiling at each other.

Cousins Beach Day – My sister and I take the kids to the beach every summer. (I create a lot of traditions involving the beach. It's my happy place.)

Easter Egg Hunt – Every year my family gets together to celebrate Easter with a big meal and an Easter egg hunt. It's a fun day.

End of Summer Beach Day – We pack all our beach gear into the trunk one more time on that last weekend before school starts and send off summer with a bang.

December Birthdays – My husband and two of our friends have birthdays within a week of each other. So we get together at our house for some food and music to celebrate.

Draw Names for Christmas – I mentioned this in the Fall Potluck. My side of the family draws names for Christmas. We've had fun coming up with creative gift ideas each year. There were a few years where the gift had to fit inside of a stocking. One year we did a white elephant exchange with gift cards. One year we swore not to ask for ideas, but almost everyone cheated, and one year we each donated to a charity in honor of the person whose name we drew.

Family Recipes – Pass down family recipes to your kids. The spaghetti, chili, and dumplings that I make are the recipes I grew up on with some tweaking here and there.

Christmas Eve – We typically go to candle light service on Christmas Eve. And when I was growing up, we opened one gift on Christmas Eve.

Special Plate – Serve dinner or dessert on a special plate on birthdays or special occasions.

Sunday Supper – Cook a big dinner after church and invite friends and family… whoever can come, come, and make it a standing invitation.

Weekend Picnics – Enjoy lunch or dinner in the park or in your backyard.

Saturday Bike Rides – This is one of those traditions that I have romantic notions about. *(Is it just me, or does bike riding around town have a certain appeal?)* But I've never initiated it, mostly because I'm so short that it's hard to find a bicycle that I can ride comfortably. So I end up pedaling the way Forrest ran, with all that I have in me, only to tire out and realize I've only pedaled a few feet.

Movie Night – Pop popcorn, buy some movie candy, and see what's on Netflix or Amazon Prime. Walmart has a bin full of dollar movie candy and another bin right next to it full of $5 DVDs. The selection is actually decent.

Game Night – Take turns playing your favorite games. This is another one that I dream of but haven't started, except during Fall Family Potluck.

Family Read Alouds – This is a great opportunity to read the classics or favorites from your childhood with your kids or grandchildren.

Service Projects – Pick a charity to support and periodically volunteer with them or serve on a service project at church. The day my daughter and I volunteered to help fill boxes of food for The Hunger Project was one of the most rewarding bonding experiences we've had together.

Fall Hayrides – Bring in the Christmas season with a hayride on a Christmas tree farm and pick out your tree or buy some greenery.

Bedtime Stories – Make them up, do a little oral storytelling, or read your favorite children's books. Some of my favorite memories are of hearing fits of giggling (from both my husband and daughter) from my daughter's bedroom during bedtime stories.

> *Tip: If you're an introvert, keep hosting to a minimum, entertain small crowds, or even host at an alternate location so that you can go home to a clean, quite space and rejuvenate. Extroverts, party on!*

The time together and memories created will without a doubt add richness and fullness to your life. That sounds soul-nourishing to me.

So far, we've talked about creating a home that loves you back in relation to memories and everyday life. Now we're going to embark on a journey towards nurturing our enthusiasm and passions.

CHAPTER 7

What's the Occasion?

My mom and I were packing the Ironstone dishes and Fiestaware I'd chosen from my grandmother's collection when I commented, "No one sets a formal table anymore."

"Well, they should," my parents answered in unison.

Hearing my parents talk about the beauty of a table setting sparked a desire in me to do this more often.

So, once I got the dishes home, I unpacked them and set the breakfast table, just because. My daughter happened to notice and commented that she liked it, saying it made her feel special and gave her something to look forward to.

Looking at the table, I understood what she meant; a set table, in and of itself, is a special occasion. There really doesn't need to be a special occasion to enjoy the good stuff. So set the table.

- Use your cloth napkins and the good dishes.
- Wear your "nice" clothes to run errands.
- Burn the "decorative" candles.
- Play your favorite party music.
- Fix a fancy meal.
- Drink the good wine.
- Eat dinner in the dining room.
- Use the monogrammed hand towels.
- Wear the expensive perfume.

Don't put off until tomorrow what you could enjoy today. It will change the way you feel about home.

CHAPTER 8

Conclusion – The Wanting

I HOPE THAT this section of the book has painted a picture of what home can be, especially if you've thought of home as just a place to land at the end of the day or as temporary or ordinary.

Knowing what a home can provide is the first step in creating a home with purpose.

So before you move on to the next part of the book, take some time to complete the following exercises.

Tip: *You are far more likely to succeed if you write it down. So, grab a piece of paper and record your answers.*

Describe how you want your home to feel, IE – warm, comfortable, inviting.

Describe how you want to feel in your home, IE – safe, confident, strong, capable.

Is your home a place that fosters those feelings?

If not, what changes can you make in your home?

What is your motivation for making the necessary changes? IE – to enjoy coming home after work, to create a nurturing environment for your family, to reduce stress.

Our environment has a lot to do with our mindset. So in the next section of the book, we will address what is likely the biggest factor in how we feel about our homes – clutter.

PART 2

Clearing the Clutter

"Clutter is nothing more than postponed decisions."

Barbara Hemphill

CHAPTER 9

The Importance of Organizing

A HOME THAT NURTURES is organized, and I believe getting organized is a very necessary step in creating a nurturing home. So I've asked professional organizer and author of *From Hoarding to Hope,* Geralin Thomas, to share her thoughts and tips on the importance of organizing.

Here's our interview:

Q. How does organization, or lack thereof, affect us in our homes?

A. Clutter and disorganization can affect your wellbeing in a number of ways, including damaging your health and making you feel completely stressed and overwhelmed. However, I think the financial costs of a cluttered home are the most far-reaching. Here are just a few ways clutter can negatively affect your budget:

Missed deadlines

Damaged valuables

Duplicate purchases

Storage rentals

Q. For those struggling to get started or overwhelmed by the process, can you suggest where and how to get started?

A. The best way to prevent feeling overwhelmed with a big organizing project is to break it up into what I like to call "Tiny Tasks." Start with a small area, like a portion of your kitchen counter or the coffee table in your living room. Work to organize that one spot and maintain it for a few days. Small accomplishments will help to motivate you to continue on your journey toward organization.

Q. What are your favorite resources for organizational supplies?

A. I love everyday items that make managing modern life easier. Here are a few of my favourite examples:

Wall-mounted magnetic bars can hold anything from kitchen knives to kids' toys.

<u>Small decorative bowls placed throughout the house store keys, watches, and loose change.</u>

Desk organizers are a must have for every home office and create unique spaces for office supplies.

<u>Color-coded tabs identify which cables to go with which electronics and help tame cord chaos.</u>

Magazine folders hold much more than magazines, including mail, kids' homework, or documents you need to file or scan.

A few of my favorite apps are – Dropbox, MyFitnessPal, Mint, BrightNest, Evernote, AroundMe, Hipmunk and Unroll.me.

Q. When looking for inspiration, is there a particular thing you do to get inspired?

A. When I want to feel inspired, I seek out creative ideas. Organizing systems need to serve a functional purpose, but they should also be beautiful and easy to use. I'm always inspired by the work of interior designers. A few of my favorites include – Jan Showers, Phoebe Howard, and Mary MacDonald.

Q. What has brought you to this point in your career? And what is your advice for people looking to follow in your footsteps?

A. My best advice is, don't be afraid to hire an expert. Investing money to hire a team of experts to do what you don't want to do or can't do can save you money and a lot of stress. For example, if you want to appear more professional on your website and blog, hire an editor or copywriter to check over your writing. Or if it would take you two days to do what an accountant could do in a few hours, hire the professional and stay focused on what you love doing.

Q. Thank you, Geralin, for sharing your tips with us. Before you go, would you please share your top 5 picks for organizing products?

A. Top 5 Picks:

Mirrored magazine rack - for holding magazines and books.

Decorative bowls - to hold watches, keys, rings, or loose change.

Tiered tables - perfect for small spaces.

Gorgeous trays - make it easier to lift things and clean under or around items.

Bamboo bar carts - They're versatile and can be used in any room of the house. Imagine using one as a nightstand or putting it in the bathroom to hold lotions, potions, and towels.

Those are some very helpful and insightful answers! It's apparent from the interview that clutter and organization are a pair; clutter is the problem and organization is the solution.

<u>Decluttering is the first step towards solving the clutter problem</u>. So, join me in the next chapter and we'll get started.

CHAPTER 10

The 4-Part Decluttering Method

I LOVE ORGANIZING! Even so, I have problem areas in my home, the behind-the-closed-doors areas, that I'm still working on. Those areas, without a doubt, cause stress, duplicate purchases, missed deadlines... all the things Geralin mentioned in the last chapter.

In fact, because of a cluttered desk, I broke two light bulbs and had to dig through the mess to find something I needed. *It was stressful to say the least.*

Every time that I passed by my desk, which was often, I felt burdened and stressed, and my mind felt cluttered. That visual clutter had a trickledown effect, creating emotional and mental clutter.

Once I finally cleared off the desk, I felt better – relieved, calm, and glad. And then the following morning the first thing Mr. Hines and our daughter noticed was the desk.

Before we move on, I want you to complete this exercise:

Look at the "before" picture of my desk and take mental notes of how it makes you feel.

Seeing this stresses me out all over again!

Now look at the "after" photo of the same area on the desk and describe how it makes you feel.

Once the desk was organized, I had room for my computer and the space to think freely and creatively. So worth the effort *and maintenance*!

There is a four-step method I use when decluttering any space in my home, and I believe this method will work for you as well.

How to Declutter Your Home

1: Gather 5 containers. You can use cardboard boxes, laundry baskets, plastic trash bags, or a combination, just as long as you have a way to collect items in each category.

2: Label the containers – Trash, Keep, Recycle, Donate, and Lost & Found.

3: Pick a space to declutter. I recommend starting small such as with a kitchen drawer, your nightstand or a small closet.

> *Tip: If you are decluttering a room, start in one corner and work clockwise. If you're clearing out the cabinets under the kitchen or bathroom sink, work left to right. And, for clearing out closets, work from top to bottom.*

4: Sort everything you touch into one of those 5 containers, following these guidelines:

- **Trash** it if it is broken or too heavily worn to donate. Before you throw away expired or unused medications, the FDA advises you to mix them with something unpalatable like kitty litter, then seal it in a plastic bag. Your waste management company may also have or know of a take back program.

- **Donate** it if the item is in good shape but you don't love it or use it.

- **Recycle** batteries, chemicals, electronics, paint, etc. Contact your local waste management company to find out how to properly dispose of them.

- **Keep** what you use and/or love. Base this decision on your priorities and on the lifestyle you're creating.
- **Lost & Found** – Put any misplaced items you find in this container. The "other" sock, missing toys, loose change, remote controls, etc... Wait to return them to their rightful place lest you get distracted from the job at hand. *(I can't tell you how many times I went to put something away, only to lose an hour looking through old photos or reading greeting cards.)*

Next
- Take out the trash and schedule bulk/heavy trash pick-up for items that don't fit in the trash can.
- Arrange to have the donations picked up or take them to a donation center.
- Set your recyclables in your recycle bin for pick up or take them to a recycle center. Some centers only take certain items on certain days and fees may apply.
- Return the lost & found items to their homes.
- Clean your empty space.

Tip: Did you know that you can take papers to be shredded to places like Office Max? They charge cents on the pound, and in my opinion it's worth it to have someone else do for me what would take me an hour to do.

Keep in mind that you do not have to do all of these steps in one day. Instead, break up your projects into smaller, more manageable tasks. For example:

Day 1 – Sort and label. (If you are decluttering a large or very cluttered space, allow more time.)

Day 2 – Throw away the trash.

Day 3 – Deliver donations and recycling to designated centers.

And so on.

Decluttering is an ongoing process in our homes, so I've created a printable cheat sheet for you to have on hand. Find it in the Resources section after this chapter. I recommend printing it out and keeping it in your home management binder for easy reference.

Now we're ready to organize the "Keep" pile.

Clearing the Clutter: Resources

Printable Sorting Labels – Included in the Free Resource Guide (sharonehines.com/ResourceGuide)

The Step-by-Step Decluttering Guide– The "cheat sheet" version of Chapter 10, plus other tips such as questions to ask yourself when sorting sentimental items. (sharonehines.com/ResourceGuide)

FDA guidelines for safe disposal of medicines – This website goes into detail on the proper disposal of medications and provides printable lists. (sharonehines.com/safedisposal)

Clutter Personality Quiz – You will find this fun quiz at Geralin's blog, Metropolitan Organizing. Taking this quiz will help you identify why you create clutter. Thankfully, Geralin offers simple solutions for each clutter personality. (sharonehines.com/clutterquiz)

CHAPTER 11

5 Simple Storage Tips

ONCE YOU'VE CLEARED OUT the clutter, you are left with the keep pile we created in the previous chapter. So now that you've decided what to keep, it's time to put it all back. But first let me share some simple storage tips that will make the process go more smoothly:

- **Do sort like items together.** Hair products, paper products, medicines, makeup, baking pans, etc.
- **Wait to buy any containers** until you determine what type of containers you need. Start by taking inventory of the keep pile. Then ask yourself what type of containers will best serve

your purposes. For example, you wouldn't want to put all of your hair products in a shallow bin where they will fall over every time you remove or replace an item. (Ask me how I know.) Also be sure to measure your space to determine what size containers will fit into your space.

- **Use vertical space.** If you do not have the floor space to spread out, then use vertical space. Take advantage of wall space, the space above doors, behind doors…, etc. You'll find ideas for what to store in these vertical spaces in the next chapter.
- **Do clean your space before putting anything back**. Take advantage of the empty cabinet, shelf, floor, etc. to dust, install liners, or sweep.
- **Save money on organizing products**. Often you can find very inexpensive containers at dollar stores. You can also repurpose household items: empty food containers, trays, and dishes.

CHAPTER 12

A Place for Everything

THERE ARE SOME usual suspects when it comes to storage and organization. So, I've put together a list of ideas for the most common problem areas in organizing.

Jewelry

- Use egg cartons to hold rings, small earrings, and bracelets.
- Purchase neck forms inexpensively at craft stores or on Amazon to store statement necklaces.
- Saucer plates are great for storing everyday jewelry on your nightstand or dresser.

- Pull those crystal candlesticks out of storage and use them to stack bracelets. *(You could also use any type of bottle as long as your bracelets fit over it.)*
- Attach inexpensive cup hooks or miscellaneous knobs you might have on hand to a strip of wood to hang necklaces.
- Frame a metal grate, chicken wire, or an old screen to store earrings.

Under Cabinets

- Use stacking bins or stacking shelves to make the best use of vertical space.
- Take advantage of over-the-door space to store hair styling tools, beauty products, toiletries, foil, plastic wrap, lunch sacks, cleaning supplies, or cleaners.
- Remove products from packaging to free up space in bins and baskets.
- Use sliding drawers and lazy susans to keep items within easy reach. *(Cookie sheets can substitute as a sliding drawer.)*
- Sort pots and pans by type and nest them together, or use a stacking organizer.
- Use storage dividers for pot lids and bakeware.

- Nest plastic storage containers by size and shape.

Closets

- Use shoe pocket organizers for not only shoes, but bras, socks, tights, leggings, pantyhose... anything that will easily fit into the pockets. Be sure to label the pockets if they aren't see-through.
- Use vertical wall space to hang accessories such as scarves, belts, and caps.
- Bookcases make a great substitute for expensive shelving. You can find them very inexpensively on craigslist and in buying and selling groups on Facebook.
- Keep hangers all one color for uniformity. My favorite hangers are at the Dollar Store.

The Pantry

- Tiered organizers, lazy susans, and baskets keep food organized, visible, and accessible.
- Use an over-the-door organizer for spices, packets, baggies, lunch sacks, and other small items.

- Use the top shelves for items that you do not use every day, such as seasonal cookbooks, serving pieces, and bulk paper goods.
- Plastic rolling carts make great storage for bread items, lunch kits, chip clips, and paper goods.
- Hang a hook on the wall for your aprons.
- <u>Store like things together – pasta, breads, snacks, canned goods, baking supplies, etc.</u>
- Empty snacks out of packaging and store together in a large bin or basket.

The Garage

- Divide the space into zones, keeping the most used zones such as lawn equipment near the garage door for easy access.
- Use a 2x4 board on the floor to know when to stop the car
- Take all old paint and expired chemicals to a waste management facility. Most waste companies have a site specifically for these types of materials or have a designated drop off day.
- Designate a box for collecting items to be donated.

- Store seasonal items on overhead racks or on top shelves.
- Use a hanging system to take advantage of vertical space. It can be as simple as hooks attached to the walls (through the studs).
- Plastic hampers make great storage for pool noodles, kid toys, balls, and sports equipment.

And perhaps the most troubling of all...

Mail/Incoming Papers

- Designate a basket or tray for incoming mail.
- <u>Sort mail into</u> – <u>recycle, shred, respond. Immediately</u> drop the recycle pile into the <u>recycle bin.</u>
- Respond accordingly – RSVP, File, Bills, Hold. (We keep a V.I.P, *very important papers*, file where we save papers that we need temporarily such as ticket confirmations, itineraries, jury summons', etc.)
- Once you RSVP, write the date on your calendar, store the address and registry information (if applicable) in your phone, and throw away the invitation.
- File weekly.

- Periodically go through your Hold/VIP papers and throw away anything that has expired.
- Remove your bills from the bill folder to pay on your scheduled bill pay dates.
- Shred at least once a week.

Now that everything has been put back in place, let's talk about how to keep it that way.

CHAPTER 13

Staying Organized

THERE IS NOTHING quite like the feeling of a freshly organized space. You will literally feel the weight lifted off of your shoulders, which I find to be a great motivator for staying organized.

Any time you're putting a system in place, involve everyone in the family. This gives them a sense of ownership and pride. Once the system is set up, make sure everyone understands it. Walk them through the process, and if you have little ones, let them practice.

Once everyone is familiar with the way things are organized, the key to staying organized is maintenance. Pay attention to how your family uses the space. If a system you set in place isn't working the way you planned, tweak it to suit your family's needs.

For example, if your family always leaves their shoes by the door instead of on the shoe rack in the garage, put a basket by the door. If wallets and keys typically land on the kitchen island, *rather than on the cute hooks you bought*, use a basket or tray to contain the clutter.

Regularly go through your belongings to donate or throw away what you're no longer using and be sure to designate a day each week to shred and file.

The structure and routine of having a system in place provides feelings of comfort and security. That's what I call good home management. Actually, my favorite thought on home management comes from Helena at A Personal Organizer

She says, "Home Management goes beyond mowing the lawn and doing the laundry — that's *house* management. Home management is making sure your family's needs are met."

I love that! And I'd add that meeting the needs of your family is a sign of good home management, or what I like to call doing home on purpose. Before we move onto cleaning, I want to share a few tools and resources for staying organized.

Staying Organized: Resources

Tips for Your Organizing Style – A successful organizing system is the one that works for you. Taking this quiz will help you identify your style and stay organized. (sharonehines.com/smead)

Retail Stores – I typically buy closet shelving at Home Depot. They will cut the shelving to size for you. I also like their selection of cabinet organizers. I like Target for office and desk organization. And I've found baskets, bins, hampers, hooks, kitchen organizers, and more at Ross, Marshall's, TJ Maxx, and HomeGoods. The Dollar Store has the best slim velvet hangers.

How Long Should I Keep It? Free Printable – From receipts, to insurance records, to tax returns, to birth certificates, this printable tells you how long to keep incoming papers. Print it here:
sharonehines.com/cleanmama

Setting up a Filing System – There are some good ones out there, but I settled on a DIY version of the Freedom Filer Filing System (sharonehines.com/freedomfiler). Whatever system you use, make sure it is one that fits your organizing style. You may need to make tweaks and adjustments or even combine your favorite components from each system to create one that works for you.

More Hours in My Day – by Emilie Barnes. A friend introduced me to this book when my family was just getting started, and I lived by it.

Sharon E. Hines – For decluttering tips, storage solutions and space planning ideas, visit my blog at sharonehines.com/category/home-organizing

PART **3**

Keeping It Clean

"My idea of housework is to sweep the room with a glance."

Erma Bombeck

CHAPTER 14

Greasy Stove Tops and Black Flip Flops

TRUE STORY

Once upon a time, I threw a fit.

"I'm not the maid," I declared. "No one appreciates me," I cried as I ran to get my purse and keys. *(I needed a time-out.)*

I looked down and, realizing I was barefoot, wondered, *"What if I want to browse in Target?"* So, I went to my closet, fumbled through the shoe organizer, and pulled out my black flip-flops.

"Crap, these shoes don't match my dress. My outfit won't coordinate," I thought to myself. (*You can take the girl out of the '80s, but you can't take the '80s out of the girl.*)

I decided it was insignificant considering the circumstances and slid my bare feet into the black flip-flops. I marched out of the closet and headed through the bathroom to the bedroom door where Mr. Hines intercepted me.

I yelled. He talked.

I cried. He listened.

I let it all out, telling Mr. Hines about the greasy stove top, and changing the sheets, and making the bed, and putting away laundry, and keeping a clean home, and reminding him that I work, too.

In the distance, I heard the clinking of dishes being put away. Then the whirring of the vacuum cleaner. *My daughter was doing her chores.* I started to calm down.

Then Mr. Hines said something about all of us cleaning together on Saturdays and how it won't take that long if we all work together. I felt relief, *hope even*.

I need my house to be clean. We all do. The truth is, I'm not sure why I avoid cleaning so much. Most tasks only take fifteen or so minutes and can be incorporated into a typical morning or evening routine. Not to mention I love the look and feel of a clean home.

CHAPTER 15

The Goldilocks Approach to Cleaning

We all have different versions of clean. When I lived on my own, it was "picked-up." As a young stay-at-home mother, it was "spotless." When I worked outside of the home, the goal was "clean enough." And, now that I'm a work-at-home mom, it's "tidy." I can even define them:

Picked up – Keeping your belongings put away with little to no actual cleaning involved.

Spotless – Sticking to a cleaning schedule and making sure every surface is not only clutter free, but also sparkling clean. *"Deep cleaning included,"* said in my best commercial sponsor voice.

Clean Enough – Keeping your belongings put away and cleaning only the necessities… like toilets and sinks.

Tidy – Having an organization system in place for belongings, mail, and other incoming papers. Maintaining a morning and evening cleaning routine that includes making the bed, sweeping, and regularly cleaning counter tops, sinks, tubs and toilets. Rare to occasional deep cleaning.

My expectations evolved with each stage of life, but they didn't necessarily reflect my priorities or goals. The picked-up version of clean that I settled for during my single days left me wanting. I never quite felt comfortable in my own home. My "spotless" days left me feeling guilty over not spending enough time playing with my daughter. There was a constant visual reminder of to-do lists and a longing for more cleaning efficiency during the "clean-enough" stage *a la* "Greasy Stove Tops and Black Flip Flops."

But "tidy"? Tidy has turned out to be *just* right for me, which leads me to what I call the "Goldilocks approach to cleaning" – trying different routines to see what works for you. Figure out how you can tweak a system to fit your lifestyle by asking yourself 3 simple questions:

- What doesn't work?
- What does work?
- And, in both cases, why or why not?

You'll discover the answers to these questions as you observe your household's habits, eventually landing on a system that's "just right."

Some of you will prefer one big cleaning day, others will want to tackle one cleaning task a day. The ultimate goal for everyone is being able to keep your home from feeling like a burden because you see a to-do list every time you walk into a room. Whatever your approach, it should leave you and your family feeling satisfied and comforted. Clean until your home makes you smile.

A great way to maintain your clean home is to establish a routine. I'll show you how in the next chapter.

Chapter 16

Creating a Cleaning Routine

To make your own schedule, I recommend writing down everything that you want to accomplish in a week. Then plug those tasks into a weekly calendar, making sure it fits into your schedule and lifestyle.

Once you have your routine planned, keep it in your planner or hang it in the command center.

Here is the routine that I have settled on to help me maintain a tidy home.

Morning Routine:

- Stretch
- Dress for the day
- Clear the bathroom counter of toiletries, makeup, and medications
- Wipe the bathroom sinks
- Put away pajamas and clothes
- Make the bed
- Do 1 load of laundry
- Eat breakfast
- Clear away dishes and kitchen counter clutter, IE – the toaster, condiments

Going through this routine reduces visual clutter and frees my mind to work from home during the day. My daughter gets home from school around three o'clock in the afternoons and Mr. Hines gets home by five-thirty most evenings. Then our evening routine begins.

Evening Routine:

- Check and sort the mail
- Prepare dinner
- Clean up the kitchen after dinner, including

wiping down appliances, wiping the counters, sweeping the floor, loading and washing the dishes
- Clean sweep the common areas for personal belongings
- Sweep the living room floor

The peace of mind of waking up to a fresh slate is so worth the ten to fifteen minutes it takes to do a little cleaning and putting away at night.

Now that the house is clean and organized, just take a moment to look around. It is such a freeing feeling, isn't it?

Right now, you're encouraged, motivated, and inspired. Just remember that if you want to keep that momentum going, you need to maintain what you've accomplished. I can't tell you how many times I've let the bathroom go for weeks or made a mess of a once-organized space. If that happens to you, forgive yourself, keeping in mind that we're striving for consistency, not perfection.

Then consider the behaviors and circumstances that led to getting off track. Was there a schedule change, an illness? Once you have evaluated the reasons, make the necessary adjustments to your routine.

> ***Bonus:*** *Get a printable, editable version of my routine in the Resources section of the next chapter.*

CHAPTER 17

Cleaning Tips and Tricks

NO MATTER WHAT your cleaning routine, we could all use a few tips and tricks to speed up the process. Here are a few of my favorite tips.

Drip Dry – Swish the toilet, then let the brush drip dry by propping it underneath the toilet seat. ~ *"How to Clean Toilets Like a Pro" by Denise, a reader at onegoodthingbyjillee.com*

Bar Keepers Friend – If years of use has left you with scratches on your dishes, use Bar Keepers Friend to remove them. It is a gentle abrasive that comes in powder or liquid form. You can find it in the cleaning aisle.

Microfiber Cloths – Use microfiber cloths for mirrors and stainless steel, or any other surface. They are super absorbent and don't leave streaks on shiny surfaces. I'm gradually making the switch from paper towels, making sure that the cloths are separated by use.

Dust from top to bottom – working your way clockwise around the room.

Dust Ceiling Fans – using a pillow case to wipe the blades, catching the dust inside the case. ~ *realsimple.com*

Pumice Stone – This last tip was shared with me by my former cleaning lady. I'd pointed out a hard water stain in my bathtub that I just couldn't get rid of. After she'd been working in the bathroom for a while, I heard her call my name. When I arrived, she pointed out that the trouble spot was gone.

Her secret weapon was a pumice stone. You can use it to remove hard water stains from tubs and toilets without scratching the surface. *(Unfortunately, I no longer have the luxury of hiring a maid. As my daughter would say, "Goals.")*

Create a Cleaning Kit — I prefer to keep cleaning supplies handy in bathrooms and kitchens. Then I store general household cleaners, rags, extra spray bottles, and refills in a central location such as my hallway linen closet.

DIY Cleaning Recipes — If you enjoy making your own cleaning products, I have created printable recipe cards for you to download and store in your cleaning caddy or home management binder. You'll find them in the Resources section at the end of this chapter.

Keeping It Clean: Resources

Cleaning Recipe cards included in the Printable Resource Guide (sharonehines.com/ResourceGuide)

Cleaning Routine included in the Printable Resource Guide (sharonehines.com/ResourceGuide)

Daily Routine included in the Printable Resource Guide. For the Cleaning and Daily routines, be sure to turn the paper orientation to landscape and then save as a Microsoft Word (.docx). Once downloaded, you'll be able to edit the charts to suit your routine. (sharonehines.com/ResourceGuide)

One Good Thing by Jillee - This blog also covers health and beauty and money saving tips, but cleaning is my favorite topic here.

(onegoodthingbyjillee.com/category/homekeeping/cleaning)

Clean Mama – A great resource for cleaning tips, green cleaning recipes, and cleaning printables. (cleanmama.com)

PART 4

Time and Energy

"Time is the most valuable coin in your life. You and you alone determine how that coin will be spent."

Carl Sandburg

CHAPTER 18

Beating Procrastination

WE PROCRASTINATE for all kinds of reasons. I waited until the last minute to start building my potting bench because I knew it would be difficult. I put off writing this book because I was afraid of failure. I regularly avoid cleaning because I dread it. I postponed starting a business because I couldn't decide what to do, and sometimes I waste hours on Facebook because I'm overwhelmed at all there is to do.

Does this sound familiar? Just know that you are not alone and that it *is* possible to beat procrastination.

Let's start by identifying several underlying reasons for procrastinating:

- Difficulty
- Fear
- Dread
- Indecision
- Overwhelm

These are the real obstacles we need to confront if we want to create a home that nurtures and inspires us to live a life we love. But how? Some of the best tips I've found on beating procrastination are:

Break large projects down into smaller, more manageable tasks. If you write "paint the bookcase" on your to-do list, it is far more likely to get put off than if you plan out the project and write the steps on your to-do list like this:

- Day 1 – Pick out paint.
- Day 2 – Clear off the bookcase and wipe it down.
- Day 3 – Sand and paint.
- Day 4 – Seal it.
- Day 5 – Put items back on the bookcase.

Renew Your Mind – Renewing your mind is a daily, sometimes hourly or minute-by minute, exercise, depending on when negative thoughts and self-doubt arise. Replace those thoughts with positive ones. So when thoughts like, *"Your book will fail"* creep into your mind, replace it with *"It's better to be in the ring and lose than to never be in the ring at all,"* or replace *"I hate doing laundry"* with *"I love the sound of the washing machine and the scent of detergent filling my home."*

Go With What You Know. If you're not quite sure where to start, begin with the obvious – using the location of electrical outlets or cables to determine where to place lamps, the television, etc.; removing what doesn't belong in a room; getting rid of what you don't use or love..., etc. Once you do, you will gain motivation and momentum and the next steps will become clear.

Write it Down. Write down everything that is on your mind. Once it is all written down, organize it into categories such as work, home, kids, personal, etc., and then prioritize each task. You are more likely to accomplish tasks when they are written down.

Prioritize. What must get done? What can wait? What can you delegate? And say no to anything that does not align with your priorities. Think about it this way – If you say yes to a project that doesn't fit your gifts or talents, then you are denying someone who would have been better suited for the task that opportunity. There are enough people to go around, and it *will* get done if you don't say yes. Frankly, I say shame on the people who use guilt tactics to get help.

Consider the pros and cons. If you don't do something, what will happen? Do the pros outweigh the cons? Let the pros motivate you. For example, if you don't do laundry, you will eventually run out of clean underwear. If it gets to that point, then you have to decide whether to go without, buy new underwear, or do the laundry. Do you want to get to that point? *(I don't mind telling you that I have had to make that decision and I've tried out all three options. I definitely prefer to just keep up with the laundry.)*

Let's consider another example. Dinner is over, the leftovers have been put away, and the counters wiped clean, but there are still dirty dishes in the sink (and the dishwasher is full of clean dishes that need to be unloaded and put away). If you leave the dishes for tomorrow, the consequence is waking up not only to an extra chore, but also to visual clutter. *(We talked about the negative effects of clutter in chapter 7.)*

Again, we face this decision in our household almost nightly and taking the ten minutes to just do the dishes outweighs leaving them for tomorrow. Are there times that you will just be too tired or not have enough time for the task at hand? Of course, but let that be the exception, not the rule.

Give up perfectionism. Perfectionism was a thorn in my side for most of my life. In fact, it's only as I'm writing about it that I realize my struggle with it has subsided. Perfectionism is rooted in insecurity and manifests as the need to people please, dependence on performance-based approval, performance anxiety, being critical of yourself and of others, caring what other's think, setting unrealistic expectations, and even depression.

I used to think that if I was going to be a stay–at-home mom, I'd better have the perfectly cleaned, organized, and decorated house to show for it. I secretly loved and lived for the praise and compliments over my efforts.

Then when I returned to teaching, I believed that I had to do it all – all the housekeeping, cook dinner every night, look put-together, write creative lesson plans, be loved by my students and their parents, be a present wife and mother, *all without help*.

I'll share more about how that worked out for me later in the book. The point I'm trying to make right now is that perfection is an unrealistic ideal and has no place in a nurturing home. It sets us up for failure, and fear of failure is one of the reasons we procrastinate. Once you accept that your home will always be a work in progress and that you can't do it all, you'll be much happier.

I think the biggest motivator for beating procrastination is to stop the guilt and shame that goes along with it. Sometimes unmade beds and stray belongings still bother me, but overall, I have experienced great progress and self-improvement by implementing these strategies, and you can too.

CHAPTER 19

Establishing Priorities

IN THE LAST CHAPTER, I mentioned that procrastination and perfectionism got the best of me. The truth is, *I* got the best of me by ignoring warning signs and not living according to my priorities. At that time, my number one priority was to take care of my family, home, and health. However, those were the most neglected areas of my life.

I'll share my story soon, but first I want you to stop and think about your story. When you imagine living a fulfilled life, what does that look like?

How does that life compare to reality? What is keeping you from living the life you want, from living according to your priorities?

Write down your priorities and keep them in mind as we move onto the next chapter where we'll discuss one of the biggest dream thieves.

Chapter 20

Taking Back Time

Is TIME, OR LACK THEREOF one of the things you think of when you consider what's getting in the way of living the life you want? We get so busy and feel like there isn't enough time in the day, but the truth is this – We all have the same amount of time in a day and how we spend it is up to us. I firmly believe we all have time for the things we *want* to have time for. It's a matter of choice and priority.

Real talk, your life's dreams will likely come to a standstill until you learn how to use your time wisely. Fortunately, that is what this chapter is all about.

First, you need to let go of the idea of doing it all. That is not the goal. The goal of productivity is to spend time on the things that matter, the things that bring you closer to realizing your dreams. Those things that *don't* matter become time wasters and roadblocks to productivity.

Some common ones, and the solutions, are:

Excuses – You're always going to be able to come up with a reason why not. Those reasons are just excuses in disguise, and excuses lead to procrastination.

The solution – Now is a good time to refer to Chapter 18 and pinpoint not only why you procrastinate (the excuses), but also how you procrastinate. What are your time wasters? Distractions? Write down your answers.

Physical Clutter – To set ourselves up for success, we *need* to clear the clutter. It's difficult to accomplish any task with a cluttered space and, more importantly, a cluttered mind.

The solution – Clear surface clutter daily during your morning and evening routines.

Mental Clutter – Mental clutter is all the thoughts, worries, and stresses that take over your mind and keeps you from being able to think clearly.

The solution – Clear your mind by writing down everything that is preoccupying your thoughts. This is not a list of priorities or even a to-do list. It's simply a mind-clearing exercise, so write down everything – phone calls, appointments, errands, chores, projects, relationships, commitments, emails... *(We're going to come back to this list in a moment.)*

Distractions – I've done it. You've done it. We've all done it. Wasted away hours browsing the internet, looking at Pinterest, checking in on Facebook, and looking up houses for sale even though you're not in the market to buy a new house... *(Or is that last one just me?)*

The solution – Step away from the computer, turn off your phone, and just be. This reduces stress, clears your mind, and helps you stay present for the task at hand.

Tip: When you notice yourself getting easily distracted (daydreaming, frequently checking your phone, losing your place), take that as your cue to take a break.

Email – Oh, email! It's part of the distractions trap, but it warrants its own place on the list because it creates mental clutter and can be a real time waster, a double threat.

The solution – Some of the best advice I've received on controlling email came from training during my brief stint as a Stella and Dot stylist, which I believe was based on the book *Getting Things Done* by David Allen. So, let's get started.

If you have email backed up from months, delete them. Don't read them, just press delete. *If they were important, you would have figured that out by now.*

Then, to keep your inbox in control, clear it daily by sorting it through one of these four filters – **delete, do, delegate, and defer**

- **Delete** junk email.
- **Do** anything that requires a quick action on your part. Take the minute or so to respond.
- **Delegate** it to someone else in your household or job who is better equipped to respond to the email. Simply forward it to them.
- **Defer** any email that will require more than a minute or so to respond. Save it to a folder and address it when you have more time.

You might also consider creating separate email accounts for work and home.

When I was teaching, I used to check my work email first thing in the morning. Inevitably, I would get caught up in a parent's concern and spend the rest of my morning preparation time trying to address it. One day, my principal gave me some very freeing advice.

She told me that I didn't need to start my day with someone else's agenda, that answering emails could wait until it was convenient for *my* schedule. So set aside time in your day when it's convenient for *you* to check email. Convenient meaning that you have the time to properly address each email.

Now for the rest of the things on that list you made. Pull things from it to add to your calendar and to-do list, which leads us to the next roadblock.

Failure to Plan – In my opinion, the only calendar or planner that works is the one you use. So whether you prefer apps and digital calendars or good old pen and paper, you are more likely to stick with a method that you like. Regardless of what method you use, make sure your to-do list:

- **Is realistic.** You can't do more than you have time for. So, keep track of how long each task will take. This will keep your list from getting too long and from being filled with unrealistic expectations.
- **Incorporates time blocking**. One of the skills I learned when I worked as a waitress was to

consolidate. In the restaurant business, that meant making the most of your trips to the kitchen while taking care of your section rather than going back and forth for each table.

In life, it means organizing your time so that you aren't all over town running errands or making multiple trips to the grocery store.

Look at the "given" responsibilities in your week – kids activities, volunteer duties, church, and club or group activities, then plan around that. For example, when my daughter was in tumbling, I would drop her off, then do my household shopping in the shopping center next door.

- **Focuses on the important rather than the urgent.** This is what the author of the book *Eat That Frog* refers to as, well, a frog – that one task that has the most effect on your productivity, that no one else can do and that has the biggest return on your time investment…, but that you keep avoiding or putting off. Do it and do it first thing in the day. That way, if you get nothing else done on your list, you've still had a very productive day.
- **Is relevant.** You will live an unfulfilled, unhappy life if you don't live according to your

priorities. I encourage you to take time to think about what is most important to YOU. Then determine how much time and energy you need to devote to those priorities. And ask yourself, *"Do I need to be the one to carry this out?"* In other words, what can you delegate? What can you say no to? Do you need to give up some responsibilities to make more time for your priorities?

There should be no guilt in saying no and no shame in delegating. In doing so, you buy back your time, getting to spend the time you would have been cleaning, organizing, mowing, cooking, volunteering, etc. on something that you enjoy. Your home gets what it needs to function well, and you've contributed to someone's business.

If you cannot afford to hire those services, delegate household responsibilities amongst the family or barter with a friend, IE – cook meals for the week in exchange for yard work.

Is specific. This is particularly helpful with big projects. "Organize the garage" is too vague and overwhelming. So, break big projects down into small, manageable tasks and write them as actionable items. For example, "pick out paint colors" vs. "paint colors."

- **Has unscheduled time**. Leave room in your day for the unexpected or unplanned.
- **Is forgiving**. Give yourself permission to leave things unfinished. No one gets it all done in a day. Resolve to make the most of your time, and then pick up where you left off the next day.
- **Includes personal time** – I have a section on my to-do list for personal time, but I find that I struggle with what to include. So just in case you struggle, too, here is a list of ten ideas:

  1. Nap.
  2. Read a magazine or a chapter in a book.
  3. Listen to your favorite podcast.
  4. Try a new hairstyle.
  5. Have a glass of wine.
  6. Talk to a friend.
  7. Watch your favorite show.
  8. Soak in the bathtub.
  9. Make your favorite salad for lunch.
  10. Rock on the porch or sit outdoors.
  11. Or anything that relaxes and rejuvenates you.

As you go through your day, pay attention to those things that tend to get you off task. Then work to eliminate those distractions. That might mean putting your phone on silent, closing the Facebook tab on your computer, or writing a to-do list before bed, but you'll be much more present and productive without those distractions.

CHAPTER 21

Energy Crisis

OUR HEALTH AND HAPPINESS have everything to do with how we manage our homes, our relationships, and our roles in life, but so many of us neglect to take care of ourselves.

We make New Year's Resolutions with plans to exercise and eat right, then laugh it off or excuse it away when we stop short. My opinion is people really do not take self-care seriously enough, nor do they realize the repercussions of neglecting it. *I didn't...*

My husband had been either unemployed or underemployed for about fourteen months, so we were trying to make ends meet on my teacher salary. Because Mr. Hines' last job was working as a children's pastor, we were also between churches.

I had additional responsibilities at work that were incredibly burdensome. I often worked late, sometimes not getting home until nine o'clock at night. Between work and home, I felt the weight of the world on my shoulders, and it showed.

I had trouble sleeping, regular bouts with kidney stones and gall stones, and was chronically late to work. In fact, within the first six weeks of the school year, I had used all ten of my sick days. I was living in crisis mode, and when I came home from work, I had nothing left to give.

Once my husband started working again, I lasted about three weeks before I completely crashed. The weight I was carrying came crumbling down around me, and I went down with it, reaching a point where I could not function at work any longer and quit.

At first, I was embarrassed and ashamed, not wanting to tell anyone. I tell you this because most of us, especially women, have a very hard time putting ourselves above others, taking care of other's needs to our own neglect. So I want you to really hear what happened next. When I went back to the school to collect my personal belongings, the school counselor told me that putting my foot down and saying no to the way things were was bold and right, no matter what others thought. It was just the affirmation I needed.

Then came the long, hard road of recovery through doctor visits, counseling, communication, and forgiveness. Quite frankly, it was a necessary road that opened my eyes to changes that had to be made in me, in my home, and in my relationships.

Looking back, I can see that I took on far more responsibility than I should have. I carried other's burdens and fought battles that were not mine to fight. Sometimes I still mourn over that time period in my life, the mistakes I made, the loss, but I do know that beauty was born from those ashes and that God will use my story to help others.

You cannot expect to run on empty and still have the energy and strength that is required to create a nurturing home. So pay attention to the things that drain your energy – work, worry, stress, relationships, lack of routine, clutter, poor health, debt... and take steps toward change.

SHARON HINES | 100

Taking care of yourself is one of the most selfless things you can do.

Be bold.

CHAPTER 22

Tips for Taking Care of Yourself

SLEEP – Remember when I said I was sleep-deprived? I was literally falling asleep at work and behind the wheel. After undergoing a sleep study and following up with a sleep doctor, I learned a little something about sleep hygiene. You need to:

- Keep your room cool.
- Lower your body temperature. (Taking a bath 90 minutes to 2 hours before bedtime can help with this.)

- Block out as much light as possible. A dark room promotes more restful sleep.
- Unplug from the television and all electronics at least thirty minutes before going to bed.
- Create a bedtime routine such as turning down the lights, turning off electronics, and taking a bath to signal your brain that it's time to unwind.
- Go to bed at the same time every night.
- Rise at the same time every day, even on days off.

Diet – The word "diet" in general promotes a short-term mentality; instead I am referring to the way you eat and what you put into your body, not a weight loss plan. If you want the long-term benefits of health, energy, and fitness, then lifestyle changes may be in order. I personally believe that this is best achieved by:

- **Listening to your body**. Our bodies have "tells" for what we need to add or eliminate. Pay attention to cravings, reactions to food (such as pain, bloating, or allergy symptoms), sleep patterns, and appetite. Keeping a log of what you eat and how you feel afterwards will help you and your doctor identify what changes to make.

- **Keeping a balance.** In other words, don't be so strict that you can't enjoy a slice of birthday cake or a glass of wine. *(I mean, who wants to completely give up bacon?)*

- **Reducing as much refined and processed food** from your diet as possible not because of the fads, but because they are laden with chemicals and fillers that are foreign to our bodies. Our bodies don't know how to break them down, and we end up with fat, low energy, allergies, and other medical problems. *(Keep in mind that I am neither a nutritionist nor a doctor. These are my beliefs according to my own research.)*

- **Staying hydrated.** Hydration promotes energy. If I'm feeling lethargic, I try drinking more fluids. Now, here's how I approach it. I don't tell myself that I cannot have Dr. Pepper or sweet tea. Instead, I just make sure to drink water, too, making it more palatable by drinking it at room temperature and sometimes adding lemon or mint. Create a plan that works for you.

Take Breaks – This includes quick mental breaks at work, time for meals, time for hobbies, time for friends, time off in the evenings and on the weekends, vacations, and taking what I call little mini-vacations such as picnics, bike rides, or day trips.

Avoid drama – Always being in conflict is stressful and exhausting. What I have observed is this – The folks who continually find themselves in the midst of it are drawn to it like a moth drawn to a flame because being in the know, holding secrets, and being in control feeds our basic human need to belong.

However, how we go about filling that need can be detrimental to our mental and emotional health. If you find yourself continually in and out of conflict, take some time for introspection. It may be a good idea to see a counselor to get a clear perspective and understanding of your behavior.

Unplug – I mentioned this with sleep, but it warrants repeating. Staying connected online is a form of clutter that keeps our minds from resting, and I cannot emphasize enough that our minds **need** rest.

My husband served simultaneously as children's pastor and deacon at our former church. This meant that he was always on call, always available by phone or email. Our evenings and weekends were routinely interrupted by the ping of an email alert or text alert, or the annoying duck quack sound that my husband had set as his ring tone at the time. However, we didn't realize just how disruptive this was to our home life until we, at the advice of the senior pastor, left my husband's computer and cell phone on his desk for the entire two weeks of our vacation.

Being unplugged allowed us to truly rest and relax, and it turned out to be one of the best vacations we've ever had.

I know how hard it is to truly walk away from the job and unplug. *(Teachers are possibly the worst at it.)* But let me just say this – Whether it's difficult because we believe the office can't exist without us, because we can't exist without them, or both, we're being dishonest with ourselves. The truth of the matter is that everyone will be just fine.

Connect – We were created to be in community, so I encourage you to find your people, those people you can trust to be themselves, that will allow you to be yourself, and with whom you can do life. In my experience, there is nothing more emotionally nurturing than that.

Commune – To me, this is a little different than connect. Connecting is joining together and establishing relationships. Communing is an intimate exchange; yes, you commune with your people, but you also commune with God. I feel the most whole and feel like I can truly say "it is well with my soul" when I take the time to enter into His presence through worship and prayer.

I am a firm believer that this physical world we live in mirrors the spiritual world, meaning that if your physical condition is suffering — whether in your health, relationships, or career — the answer can be found by looking at your spiritual condition. Just a little food for thought...

Time and Energy: Resources

These resources and leaders have really helped me in the battle against procrastination and in my effort to increase productivity.

Eat Move Live 52 - by Roland and Galina Denzel. One of these days, just saying their names will be all you need. Until then, I'm very eager for you to experience two of the most gracious, practical, kind and smart health coaches I've ever had the pleasure to know. If you're health goals have alluded you up until now, this is your next step. Visit Roland and Galina at eatmovelive52.com

Eat that Frog by Brian Tracy – A great tool for overcoming procrastination, improving time management, and increasing productivity.

The War of Art by Steven Pressfield – Steven nails procrastination on the head with this book. His perspective gave me so much clarity and conviction and set me on the road to finally writing this book.

brenebrown.com – I found Brene's Ted talks on "The Power of Vulnerability" and "Listening to Shame" very encouraging. I also picked up some great nuggets of wisdom from watching a few of her interviews. (brenebrown.com)

Sharon E. Hines – 3 Ways to Calm the Chaos (sharonehines.com/calm)

PART 5

Overcoming Decorating Dilemmas

"A home should be a distillation of your interests, of who you really are. If you're happy with your life, your space will reflect that."

– Rafael de Cardenas

Chapter 23

Facing Your Fears

I BELIEVE EVERYTHING that we've focused on up to this point creates inner beauty in our homes. And if mindset, cleaning, and organizing are the inner beauty, then decorating is the outer beauty.

I like to think of it as the outfit, accessories, hair, and makeup. Just like in fashion, decorating is your chance to shine on the outside, express your style, and add personality to your home.

However, this seems to be where people get stuck, and those decorating dilemmas tend to fall into one of four categories:

Intimidation – *Is this in style? Will my friends like it? I don't have an eye for decorating.*

Undefined Style – *I don't know what my style is. I like a lot of different styles.*

Affordability – *I can't afford a designer. The furniture I want is too expensive.*

Indecision – *What if I make a mistake? What if my style changes?*

Lifestyle – *I don't have time. My kids' things have taken over. Our pets would destroy a nice couch.*

You are certainly not alone. I've been plagued by some of these very fears, too. Because of that, there is one thing I know – It is possible to overcome them.

Chapter 24

Smart Decorating Advice from a Girl Named Boog – Overcoming Intimidation

When I was in junior high, I learned that my dad had a nickname for me when I was little… – Booger, or Boog, for short.

The nickname came about because I used to hide and wait for him to come home from work. And when he walked through the door, I jumped out like a booger man.

Touched by that story, I decided that I wanted a shirt that said "Daddy's Boog" on the back. *(It was the '70s and getting sayings printed on t-shirts was so in.)*

I wore the shirt with pride until my peers started asking about it. I sensed disapproval in their questions and my pride over that shirt shrank a little.

When I'm in my house surrounded by the people and things that make it a home, I'm filled with joy and pride. I think my home is beautiful. But when I see other homes, my confidence shrinks like I'm in junior high all over again.

Can I put a room together? Yes, but I worry what others will think of it.

("Do I know what I'm doing today. No. But I'm here, and I'm gonna give it my best shot." Hansel from the movie Zoolander*)*

Do you see a theme here? Caring what others think has been a thorn in my side my entire life. Friends *(preaching to myself, but I'm sharing this because I know I'm not alone)*, we are different by design.

Different tastes, different ideas... just different. You shouldn't be so influenced by whether your friends like your couch, what the rules are, or what's in style that you are paralyzed by fear or afraid to move forward.

You don't want to be the Derek Zoolander of decorating, feeling threatened and insecure by every Hansel that comes along. The good news is that your confidence will become more like Hansel's as you discover your style.

Or maybe it's more like that girl in junior high who, even though she shrank a little on the inside, proudly told the story of how she came to be Daddy's Boog, who wore that shirt no matter what others thought.

If I could write a note to the junior high me, it would say, "Thanks for the decorating advice, Boog."

Decorate for you.

Decorate with confidence.

Create your home on purpose.

"But what if I don't even know what my style is?" Read on friends, read on.

CHAPTER 25

9 Practical Tips for Defining Your Style

For a long time, I defined my style as "Casual Elegance." Then, in the wake of Pinterest and blogs, I started to panic because my style didn't seem to fit in with what was popular, and I eventually lost my decorating confidence. So I started searching for my decorating style all over again, and I discovered some do's and dont's along the way.

Do

Create a feeling or mood. How do you want your home to feel, both to you and your guests? Warm? Inviting? Cozy? Spacious? Relaxed? Write it down.

Collect images of rooms you love, that have the look and feel you are after in your own home. You can put together a notebook or create a "My Style" board on Houzz or Pinterest.

Take note of what it is you love about each image. The color? Certain shapes? A particular texture? The way two things go together? A mood or feeling? A fabric pattern? Write it down.

Know what you don't like. This tip was advice given to me by Kathysue of Good Life of Design, and that is this — Take it a step further and write down what you don't like about the images you collected. Knowing what you don't like is just as beneficial as knowing what you do like, giving you discernment and narrowing down your options.

Decorate with what you love. My mom often says that if you love something, you will find a place for it. She is right. If you decorate with what you love and with items that evoke the mood you're after, then you will be well on your way to not only finding your style but also creating it in your home.

Trust your gut. That tip is based on advice my Aunt Marilyn gave me back in 1970-something when I was trying on a swimsuit. I kept turning and looking and looking and turning when Aunt Marilyn said, "If you have any doubts about it, don't buy it." I've lived by that advice ever since.

The bottom line is that you have instincts. Trust them.

Don't

Incorporate trends and fads – If you don't like what's "in," don't buy it. It's not going to look or feel right in your home if you don't really like it.

I bought a cow print when cows first came onto the decorating scene. *(It was like Gloria Vanderbilt jeans in junior high, I wanted a pair because everyone had them.)* I *liked* the cow print, but it wasn't really me. So, I kept moving it around from room to room, trying to force it to work, until I finally admitted my mistake and put it in the donate pile.

Buy something just because of its color — There have been so many times that I pondered (or even made) a purchase just because of its color, but color is really the last factor in making a home decor purchase. First, look for lines, shape, style, and size. If your find is also the right color, great! If not, it can be painted or recovered.

Doubt yourself — I went on a home tour and everything about the home was just gorgeous. Plaster walls, gray painted woodwork and cabinetry, white furniture… and when I left that tour, I felt like my home needed a complete makeover. *I even felt a little embarrassed of my home.*

When seeing other homes stirs up comparison and doubt, it's time to take a break from all the inspiration that is out there and focus on your own home. The doubt will settle as you find reassurance in your personal style. That assurance will eventually lead to confidence, and then you'll be able to appreciate other styles without doubting your own.

After following these do's and don'ts, I ended up right back where I started, defining my style as "Casual Elegance." It's not one of your typical style names like "French Country" or "Modern Farmhouse," but that's the beauty of it. I created my own style, one that doesn't fit into one checkbox on a style quiz.

One final thought – don't get too caught up in a name. When your style is a true reflection of you, you'll recognize it when you see it.

CHAPTER 26

Affordability: 5 Budget Decorating Ideas

WHAT I REALLY WANT you to know, *what I really want to say,* is that I don't want money to keep you from decorating your home.

I know what it is like to run out of money as soon as you pay the bills. I've experienced the disappointment of seeing something you love but not being able to buy it. And I'm all too familiar with the plans and dreams of "someday…"

Those financially challenging times have shaped the way I approach decorating, giving me some creative budget decorating ideas. Before I buy anything, *if I buy anything at all*, I shop my home, use what I have, and then redecorate. You'll be surprised at the beauty you can create using what you already have.

Redecorating has given me hope in hard (financial) times. Most of the time, that is all the room needs. But, if not, here are few more ideas:

- After you redecorate, make a note of what the room still needs. Then, **make a list and set a budget**.

- **Wait to buy** until you find what you want. Otherwise you're going to accumulate a bunch of things that end up in the donate pile.

- **Shop smart**. I always visit Ross, TJ Maxx, Marshall's/HomeGoods, or Target first. I also check online Facebook groups like Beg, Barter, Buy and Sell. You can search Facebook for a group in your area. You can also try thrift stores, eBay, Overstock.com, and craigslist. Daily deals sites are another great source. I've purchased several things from Decor Steals. There's also Antique Farmhouse, One King's Lane, and Joss & Main.

- **Repurpose** something you already own. For example, a dresser can easily be converted into a media console. A changing table or baker's rack makes a great potting bench.

CHAPTER 27

Overcoming Indecision

WHEN IT COMES to home decor, we can sometimes be plagued by indecision, spending hours, days, even weeks trying to decide.

"What if I don't like it?"

"What if I change my mind?"

The fear of making a mistake is bigger in our minds than it is in reality.

What I've come to understand as I've wrestled with indecision is that no decision is permanent. Paint can be changed, pillow covers can be switched, and accessories can be moved around. Indecision can be eliminated if you keep a few things in mind as you decorate:

Stick with your style. Keep those describing words you wrote down in Chapter 21 in mind as your make purchases. If you're trying to create an elegant, sophisticated look, don't buy home decor you describe as "cute."

Know your budget. If something is outside of your budget, then the decision is made for you. If you absolutely love it but can't afford it, you can either put it on layaway, watch for it to go on sale, or do some comparison shopping.

Wait and see. If you're uncertain about a piece, ask the store to put it on hold and then go home and wait to see how you feel about it after some time has passed. If you can't stop thinking about it and find yourself picturing several places for it, go back and get it. If a store won't hold an item, ask about their return policy. If they allow returns, go ahead and buy the item and return it if you don't like it.

Love it or leave it. If you do not love it, and it isn't at least functional, don't waste another minute thinking about it. Bringing home something you kind of like or that "will do" is like dating the wrong guy, trying to make something work that was never meant to be.

Take it home with you. Sometimes we find more than one piece we want and can't pick just one. So, buy both lamps, both comforters, or whatever the item may be, and look at them in the setting of your home. Once you decide, return the items that you didn't choose. *(Check the store's return policy before making any purchases.)*

Sample it. You can order or get samples for floors, furniture finishes, fabrics, paint, tile, etc. Bring those samples home and live with them. Look at them next to your belongings and in the lighting changes throughout the day. *Everything looks different in the lighting of your home verses in a store.* It makes the decision process so much easier.

Schedule a consultation. Sometimes we just need a second opinion. So, schedule a consultation to get a fresh, professional perspective. Whether you talk to a sales representative to get more information about a product or take advantage of in-home or virtual services, the peace of mind and time saved will be well worth it.

> *Tip: I discovered a nifty little trick once I started blogging. Photos. If you can't hire a designer, take a picture of your room. I can't tell you how many times I've either realized I*

needed to make changes, or that I shouldn't have made changes, just by looking at a picture of my space.

Remove and reverse it. Buy or sew removable pillow covers and take advantage of the versatility of slipcovers and reversible items. This allows for more options in the decision-making process.

Learn from your mistake. I've learned that paint can be changed, because I've had to repaint a room... multiple times. I now know to steer away from anything that I describe as "cute" because it is likely going to end up in the donate pile. And after that failed cow print purchase, I will stop buying trendy things just because they're popular.

Mistakes are the best learning tool out there, so don't be afraid to make one *or two*. As C.S. Lewis put it, "Experience is a brutal teacher, but you learn. My God, do you learn."

CHAPTER 28

8 Kid-Friendly Design Ideas

When Hannah was three years old, she colored all over the wall.

I overreacted.

The leather furniture was brand new when the cat scratched it.

I cried.

When my nephews were younger, they bent the metal canopy frame on Hannah's new bed.

I cussed.

Our mattress got a tear in it when we moved into this house.

I frowned.

Our bed frame broke during horseplay.

I panicked.

I've dripped paint on the floor, dinged up the walls, and dropped things that shattered into pieces. As discouraging as those moments were, it taught me a couple of things:

One, it's all just stuff and people are more important than things. And two, children and pets and accidents do not mean we can't have beautiful homes.

If you live with realistic expectations and incorporate these family friendly design ideas.

Invest in good furniture that will stand up to children, pets and heavy use. It took us awhile to save for our current furniture, but it was a very worthwhile investment. It's been eight years and our although the leather has faded, the furniture seems to get better with age.

Consider using durable finishes like washable paint for the walls, tile, and laminate or wood for the floors.

Create kid zones with bins and drawers for their belongings. Having a space to call their own gives children a sense of ownership and pride in their home.

Have a place for everything. Blankets in baskets, toys in bins, leashes on hooks, books on shelves … it keeps the stuff from taking over your home.

Use ottomans or poufs instead of a coffee table when your children are young. They can easily be moved out of the way for play time, still give babies a place to pull up as they learn to walk and are safer than the edges of a traditional coffee table.

Keep breakables out of reach of little hands. When Hannah was a baby, we had safety latches on all the cabinet doors, except the one where I kept the Tupperware. *I wish you could see the picture of Hannah asleep on the kitchen floor, surrounded by storage containers.*

Let the kids help decorate their rooms. You might end up with bright aqua walls, but it's only temporary *and you can close the door.*

Relax. This is something at which I obviously wasn't very good in my early years of homemaking. But, the frustration just isn't worth it. And at this point, I can tell you that one day you'll look back on these days with nostalgia.

CHAPTER 29

Space Planning

THERE ARE THREE THINGS to consider when planning a room.

Function

First, let's talk about function. You need to know how you will use the space to determine what pieces the room needs. Let's take my family room for example. This where we relax, eat, watch TV, visit, and entertain guests.

So, this space needed a television, plenty of seating for my family plus guests, a coffee table or ottoman, and enough end tables for everyone to have place to set their drinks.

> ***Tip:*** *It's a good idea to take your family's habits into consideration as you choose furniture and accent pieces. Since my family likes to kick up their feet, I prefer the soft surface of an ottoman over a coffee table. Placing a tray on the ottoman gives us a place to set food and drinks. When we're done, the tray can be moved, and we can use the ottoman as a foot rest.*

Focal Point

A focal point draws people in as well as anchors the room.

A room can more have than one focal point, one being where your eye instinctively travels as you enter the room. This is typically the corner directly across from the entrance of the room.

This wall is the focal point when you enter our living room from the foyer,

and the piano is the focal point as you enter the room from the hallway.

The focal point can also be the center of activity when you're in the room, such as a fireplace or an entertainment wall.

When we are in our living room, we are all about watching TV. However, I also love our vintage electric mantel, so I made them both the focal point of activity.

Flow

Next, you will need to look at the layout of the room. Where is the focal point? Where are the doors? The windows? Where does traffic enter and exit the room? Also consider the placement of cable and electrical outlets.

This will determine furniture placement. Since I tend to learn by doing, I typically just go for it, moving and arranging furniture by trial and error. If you are a visual person, you may prefer mapping out your floor plan on graph paper. There are also apps, computer software, and free online room planners available.

Whichever method you prefer, have all your measurements handy, including door openings, window sizes, and permanent fixtures such as built-ins and fireplaces. You will need these measurements to determine furniture size and placement.

As you place the furniture, make sure to:

- Leave room for traffic flow.
- Create balance. Think of a balance scale as you place furniture around the room. If you put something visually heavy (like a big or dark piece of furniture) on one side of the room, even the scale by putting something of equal weight on the opposite side of the room.

Once you have the furniture in place, you're ready to accessorize.

CHAPTER 30

Decorating Tips and Tricks

I can't tell you how many times I've stood back and stared at a room, wondering what it needed, added something, stood back and stared again. Rearranged it, stood back and stared yet again.

What am I looking for as I stand back and look? Here are a few elements:

Balance

I achieve balance by using what I call the zigzag. Let's start with color. In the first example, the colors are lined up in columns, creating a lop-sided effect.

Instead, you want to evenly distribute color throughout the vignette.

By switching the candle holder with the shell, both

the warm, golden tones and the cooler whites now zigzag throughout the vignette.

If you were to draw a line down the middle of the vignette, both the warm color and the white would be on both sides. For you mathematicians, it's like an equation – what you do to one side, you have to do to the other.

Evenly distributing the color also balances the weight of the art with the objects.

Varying Heights

These books are all the same height and don't offer enough contrast with the height of the candle holder. It's too boxy.

Replacing the shorter books with the taller ones

gives the arrangement height. When working with height, the center of the arrangement should be the tallest or highest, creating a triangle effect.

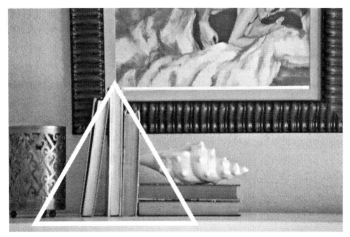

Texture

Texture creates movement and interest.

The ridges in the frame and the shell add obvious texture. The folds of the sheets in the art print and even the book pages add more subtle texture.

When adding texture to a room, consider the different textures you learned in elementary school – soft, smooth, rough, hard, bumpy.

Natural elements and fabrics are a great way to bring in texture.

Layering

Layering is just what it sounds like. Think of it like your wardrobe in cooler weather – a shirt, sweater, and scarf. In your home, throw blankets and pillows make for easy layering.

It can also be created by stacking books or setting an object on top of or in front of another.

Odd Numbers

One more decorator trick is to arrange objects in odd numbers – a single item to make a statement, or in groupings of 3 to bring balance to a vignette.

Color, shape, texture…you've got this! It's everything you learned in kindergarten.

Notes to Remember

- Achieve balance by forming a "z" or triangle with color and weight.
- Add texture and dimension through objects and layering.
- Arrange objects in odd numbers. Groups of 3 work especially well.

You can apply these techniques to styling any surface – dressers, consoles, tables, shelves, and bookcases. I offer these guidelines not to give you rules to follow, but to bring out the beauty of your belongings.

Just remember that perfection isn't the goal, and no design is without a little trial and error.

CHAPTER 31

Personalizing Your Home Decor

"Worn objects have a story to tell. They can almost seem alive with their sense of the past, especially if they show traces of human intervention."

Mark and Sally Baily

THAT IS WHAT DECORATING is all about – making your house come alive with your story and using your belongings to tell that story, not only for friends and family to enjoy, but for you, too.

I can't think of anything more nurturing that the joy you feel as you relive the moment captured in a photo, are reminded of a loved one whose dishes now fill your cabinet or feel a sense of heritage and belonging from your family monogram.

It's like a living scrapbook. But be careful *not to clutter*.

curate – *(verb) to pull together, sift through, and select for presentation. (Dictionary.com)*

With that said, here are 10 ways to personalize your home decor:

- Share things that represent your hobbies and interests. For example, if you love the beach, display a shell collection. In my own home, a vintage school bell represents my teaching career. We also keep Mr. Hines' guitar within easy reach so he can play whenever the mood strikes.

- Set out keepsakes from your childhood such as a favorite toy or game.
- Showcase inherited pieces such as dishes in plate racks or glass cabinets.
- Use your family monogram on pillows, towels, or even furniture.
- Incorporate your favorite colors in your home decor.

- Display family photos in creative ways, such as tucked in a bowl with vase filler, inside a vase or lantern, or on a table under a magnifying glass. Have your children's artwork professionally matted and framed and hang it in a gallery on the wall.

- Create a gallery wall using black and white photos of your ancestors.
- Incorporate maps from places you've lived or of favorite destinations in your home decor.
- Turn your favorite vacation photos into posters.

If a collectible, photo, or family treasure represents you in some way, consider incorporating it into your home decor.

Decorating: Resources

Blogs

- **Designed with Carla Aston** – I learn *so* much from Carla, and I highly recommend her design services if you are in the Houston, TX, area. (carlaaston.com)

- **Emily A. Clark** – Emily has great taste and is all about keeping design simple. (emilyaclark.com)

Shopping

- **Etsy** has become a favorite resource for shopping one-of-a-kind, unique and handmade home decor. It's the first place I look for throw pillow covers.

- **HomeGoods and Target** are my favorite, budget-friendly places to shop.

CHAPTER 32

Finding Home

Coming to the end of this book feels a lot like the end of a school year when I would wonder, *"Is there anything else?" "Could I have said or done more?"* The fact is, even when you've given your all, the answer to those questions is always yes. So here are some final thoughts.

It does not matter what size your house is or where you buy furniture. If you do the work, you can have a home you love and, as I like to say, that loves you back. Your home won't be perfect, but it will be good, a place where you're surrounded by the people and things you love, living a life you love.

I wrote this book because I want that for you. I believed that my wanting it for you was enough until I saw a scene from Friday Night Lights on Netflix where Coach Taylor tells one of his football players, "I can't want this for you. You're going to have to want it for yourself." In that moment, I realized my wanting it for you *isn't* enough. You have to want it too.

I'm reminded of a time when I was standing in my laundry room, taking clothes from the washing machine and putting them into the dryer. And as I did this, my mind wandered to my blog and the people who read it.

I wondered if they get it... the meaning and importance of home, the value of running a household, the need to love our homes, and the joy of having a good home. Then I thought, "If they would take my understanding and my experience and apply it, their [home] lives would be so much easier."

That is my real hope. That you will glean something of value from this book that will make the job of creating a home easier for you and help you overcome any burdens that are keeping you from having the kind of home life you want.

Think about the areas of home management where you struggle and take your time in the chapters of this book that focus on those areas, gradually implementing the strategies suggested. Creating a nurturing home is not a race or competition, so go at your own pace.

Managing a household requires continual work, but once you do the hard work of creating organizational systems, putting routines in place, and establishing order, the work becomes lighter. Then you get to reap the rewards – peace, comfort, joy, happiness, fulfillment, contentment, hope, and ultimately, finding home.

If you have questions or need help along the way, you can always find more organization ideas, cleaning tips, decorating inspiration, and life advice on my blog, Mrs. Hines' Class, at sharonehines.com.

See you there,

About the Author

A former educator with 18 years of teaching under her belt, Sharon is the wife, mother, and author behind the home and lifestyle blog Mrs. Hines' Class. There you will find organizing help and inspirational life lessons designed to help you create a home and life you love. Sharon has been featured on several online sites such as The Huffington Post and Buzzfeed and has even made a few TV appearances.

She resides in the suburbs of Houston, TX, with her husband, the family cat, Blackie the gray tabby, and Britt, the dog she got because she misses her daughter. She's proud to say her daughter is living her best life in California while studying to be a nurse. As an empty nest couple, Sharon and Matt enjoy reading on the beach, binge-watching t.v., and laughing, lots of laughing.

What's Next?

Be sure to download your free printable resources guide at sharonehines.com/ResourceGuide

Then sign up for the **Free Decluttering in a Day Challenge** at sharonehines.com/DeclutterChallenge

Made in the USA
Columbia, SC
02 May 2022